And so will the Macaroni penguins, seals, and skuas. Peace descends on the empty beaches. There are no cries of homecoming penguins, no one shrieks abuse at the passersby, no baby seal barks furiously at a penguin that has come too close. Soon snow covers the empty beach and tremendous storms thunder over the ice-covered ocean. Chinstrap penguins spend the whole winter swimming out at sea. There are vast quantities of krill to be caught, and when they are tired, they can rest on an ice floe. Cold as it is, they will never freeze in their thick, warm coats of down and feathers.

Next spring, when the sun begins to rise higher and warm the slopes of Bouvet Island, they will return to their nesting sites to bring up their new chicks with the other penguins of the colony.

The Antarctic autumn comes, with rain and snow. March means spring-time in the northern hemisphere, but here, near the South Pole, violent storms arise and rage for days. The sea is covered with foam, and mighty waves break against the coast. Even if you had a safe, sturdy house, you could not stay in the Antarctic now. There are no houses on Bouvet Island and we are glad to be able to go home to a warm, bright spring. Our ship gathers speed, heading north to warmer climates.

But the penguins stay a little longer, in spite of storm, rain and snow. Not until their children are fully adult will all the Chinstrap penguins — old and young alike — leave their island.

By the end of summer the chicks are almost as big as their parents. Under the grey down, the adult plumage has already grown, and as the tattered down falls out, the gleaming new feathers will come to light. Soon the children will be able to go out to sea and catch their own food. Only now can the parents also grow new feathers — they could not do this before because they had to catch krill for their babies.

It is February now and the chicks are almost grown up, though some of their baby down still clings to them. Sometimes two of them will quarrel, like the young Chinstrap and Macaroni penguins in this picture. They came too close and are now squawking at each other with wide-open beaks. One parent of each young penguin looks on, to make sure they do not hurt one another.

As summer passes the chicks of the Chinstrap penguin family grow larger and larger. Already they look more like adult penguins. The down on their backs darkens and they now have pretty pink feet, just like their parents. The parents seem very proud of their big, healthy children. Sometimes one of the youngsters takes a walk not too far from the nest, so that only one fledgling is left at home with its father or mother.

The father seems to have decided to enjoy his family for a little longer before he sets off for his turn.

But now he must go down to the beach, and in time he too will return with plenty of krill, because the chicks have to grow up quickly in the short Antarctic summer.

Then they scream and call again, bowing and turning their heads in uni-son. Under one of the parent penguins you can see the two chicks still like woolly balls in their downy grey plumage.

The impatient chicks are always squawking for more food. They thrust their bills deep into their mother's throat, where the regurgitated food is waiting for them.

The mother penguin is home at last! She has just reached the nest and wants to tell her family that she is there. Making herself as tall and thin as possible, she stretches her head and neck upwards and squawks loudly. Does she mean she is glad to see her family again?

The father, who has been looking after the chicks all this time, is glad to see his wife again too, and "sings" a little song. It is not easy to understand how the penguin mother manages to find her own husband among all the penguins in the huge colony. Perhaps they recognize each other by their voices, and that is why the returning penguin squawks and sings, loud enough for the sitting bird to hear: "Here comes your mate!"

The two greet each other with deep bows, which mean that each has recognized the other as its mate.

The fur seals are different. They reserve special places for themselves on the beach and attack the penguins if they come too close. Fur seals do not eat penguins but may easily injure them in their savage attacks, so the penguins keep a sharp lookout for them. The only seal they rightly fear is the spotted leopard seal that goes penguin-hunting in the water.

Fur seals also have babies in summertime — adorable babies, that play together like children in a nursery. Just like human children, they love splashing about in the water.

On their way home the Chinstrap penguins meet the gigantic elephant seals, sprawled on the beach in little groups to keep each other warm. Though they look dangerous when they open their great muzzles and roar, the penguins are not afraid of them.

When these beautiful big gulls fly over the penguin colony, their sharp eyes spy every unguarded egg, and every sick or straying chick.

Take a good look at the skua and you will find out quite a lot about its lifestyle. From its webbed feet you can see that it is a waterfowl, but the sharp, hooked bill and strong claws also show that it is a bird of prey. By living near the penguins they can always be sure of finding enough food for their own children.

They have earned a short rest before beginning the laborious trudge
back to their nesting-places somewhere in the huge penguin colony.
On the beach they meet other inhabitants of their island. Here are the
comically-named Macaroni penguins, so-called because of the fantastic
bunches of long bright feathers sprouting from the sides of their heads,
which made early explorers think of the extravagant hairstyles of the
fashionable young men known as "Macaronis" in the 18th century.
The two kinds of penguins breed together in the same colony and as
long as they all take care not to come too close to each other's nests,
they do not quarrel. So large numbers of penguins can breed on the few
convenient sites, and eggs and chicks are better protected by the many
watchful eyes in the big colony than if each pair nested on their own.
And penguin parents have good reason to be watchful, because of the
skuas...

When the penguin mothers and fathers have filled their stomachs with krill for their little ones, they return to Bouvet Island.

They are close to the shore now, but before they reach it a mighty breaker rolls them over and over and sucks them back into deep water, until they vanish altogether in the foaming surf. But they never give up, and each wave brings them a little closer to the beach.

In smooth water these penguins, which have just been flying, fishlike, through the water, become birds again, swimming with lifted heads, like ducks. When at last there is firm ground under their feet, they turn back into little upright beings in black and white suits.

But first the penguins eat until their own hunger is satisfied. Then they leap onto one of the shimmering blue ice-floes that drift about the sea like floating islands and provide a safe and comfortable resting-place. Perhaps you remember that the first penguins we saw from the ship were standing on one of these floes. Sometimes penguins slide down the smooth ice on their feathered tummies, whizzing back into the sea in a splendid tobogganing game.

Here they "fly" along under water, kept warm by a thick layer of fat
under the skin, and their dense plumage also keeps them dry and snug.
Their outstretched bodies become streamlined, and they can swim fast —
as fast and elegantly as fish.
When they shoot upwards from the foaming waves they remind us of
dolphins at play. As they leap, a thin coating of air covers their feathers,
enabling them to glide even more swiftly and easily through the water
when they plunge back again.

The penguin mother has to make the long and difficult journey on foot, although she is a bird and has wings. She has to clamber over steep, fissured rocks, passing many other families of the penguin colony on her way. Many of them are also setting out on feeding trips, and they join together in small groups.

At last one group has reached the shore. The flat rocks along the edge make a good starting point for the dive into the water. We shall soon see how they make use of their unusual wings: as they leap into the water the birds that walk upright on land like human beings turn into something quite different — much more like fish, with fins which are really bird's flippers. The sea is the penguins' natural habitat, which they leave only to brood and grow new feathers. Suddenly we realize how well they are adapted to their icy home.

The second penguin parent is returning from a fishing expedition. Let's call him the father, though in fact we can't tell the difference between them. He has satisfied his own hunger at sea and his stomach is stuffed with food for the chicks, which he will look after while their mother is away.

… the name given to the millions upon millions of small, shrimp-like creatures, which the penguins catch at sea and bring back in their stomachs to the chicks. The krill feed on plankton, the clouds of countless minute organisms that fill the seas. Krill is the main source of food for the many thousands of penguins on Bouvet Island and throughout Antarctica.

The two chicks sit comfortably on the parent penguin's feet and if they feel cold they can push their way under its warm feathers. They beg for food, nudging their parent's beak with their small black beaks and squeaking softly. Then the parent bird regurgitates — or brings up — some of the krill from its stomach and feeds the chicks.

The penguin babies have arrived! One is just peeping out from under its mother's — or perhaps its father's — tummy. It has a soft, wooly covering of light-grey down, more like the fur of a young mammal than the feathers of a bird.

All over the penguin colony the stones are covered with the white and reddish streaks of their droppings. Even the penguin parent's white shirt front is stained with red from krill…

Some of the younger penguins in the colony and those who have not found partners or are not brooding have gathered by a small pond where the seals are playing.

By now, as you see, their once-gleaming black feather evening dress looks remarkably patchy and rumpled. The rocks they stand on are thick with small feathers, for the penguins are growing a new coat of feathers. During the year the feathers become badly worn by so much swimming and diving in the salt sea water, by countless leaps ashore and back into the water, by sliding games on the ice, by wind and sun, rain and snow. Before next winter comes, the new plumage must be warm, thick and smooth again. So now, in summertime, the old feathers fall out in bunches, and underneath, the spotless, shining new feather suit is already growing. In this feather-growing period, which takes two to three weeks, the "non-breeders" simply stand around, doing nothing. They cannot go out in search of food until their new coats are watertight, or they would freeze to death in the icy water.

Now let's see how our pair of breeding penguins are getting along.

In December, at the beginning of the Antarctic summer, most of the brooding period of nearly 40 days is over. Mother and father penguin take turns on the nest, but each of them has to keep the eggs warm alone for quite a long time while the other is at sea, eating as much food as possible before coming back to the demanding business of brooding. The penguin parents have sprayed a striking star-pattern of white droppings around the stone nest — unintentionally, of course!

Penguins look much more like birds when they are lying on the nest than when they are walking upright. Only their wings are not at all like birds' wings, and they were certainly not meant for flying, since they have no wing feathers at all.

Throughout the long Antarctic winter these Chinstrap penguins have lived out in the water, among the ice-floes. In October and November, when autumn winds are tearing the leaves from the trees in the northern hemisphere, they return to their island, for this is when spring begins in Antarctica. The males arrive first and those that land earliest select the best positions for their nests. They guard their nesting sites well, driving off other penguins while they wait for their womenfolk to return from the sea. The males stretch their bodies upright, head and neck lifted high, and flap their wings, telling the others: "This is my nesting place. This is where I live!"

One day the females return from the sea and each finds her partner from the previous year. To you and me all penguins — male or female — look alike, but they recognize each other and are glad to be together again. There are no grasses or twigs on the island, so the penguins gather small stones and pebbles, building them into a walled nest. Inside this the female lays her two eggs — or sometimes only one — which look very much like hens' eggs.
Many thousands of penguins live together in one breeding colony. The nests are so close together that the penguins have only just enough room to walk between them.

We can also go right up to the penguins without alarming them. Imagine trying to do that with wild animals in your own country! They would probably run away immediately. But these cheerful birds stand calmly about on the rocks, staring curiously back at us. They are called Chinstrap penguins, because of the narrow black line that runs from the edge of their black feather caps down their cheeks and right under their chins, just like a strap keeping the black cap in place.

None of the animals has any fear of us. Most probably they have never seen a human being before — or at least none who did them any harm. So they need not regard us as enemies, but gaze trustfully at us with just as much curiosity as we feel for them — or so we imagine. What does this seal really think of the strange, two-legged creature who wishes her "Good morning"?

There are no flowers on this island – it is too cold for that. The only plants that grow here are mosses and lichens, which flourish in the rain and mist that often envelop the island. Even summer days here are more like mild winter days at home. Only on the rocky cliffs does it become a little warmer when the sun shines on them.

Flocks of sea-birds, which nest somewhere on the steep rock walls inland, fly shrieking over our heads. On the beach we meet other inhabitants of the island. Hundreds of fur seals lie at ease here and the nearest to us bark at us as we pass. Huge elephant-seals bask on the sand. Here, too, are the penguins we have come to see.

After many days at sea, Bouvet Island appears on the horizon. As we sail closer, the island looks more and more like a miniature mountain range rising straight out of the ocean. Long, long ago the island was a volcano, spewing fire, smoke and lava high into the air. Now its peak has a thick icecap and some of its glaciers reach down to the sea. Large and small icefloes drift around its coastline.

Our ship anchors offshore, in deep water. For our landing on Bouvet Island we take to an inflatable rubber dinghy that carries us safely through the foaming surf to the island's rocky shore. Steep cliffs rise sheer from the sea and in many places the waves have scoured strange towers and even a bridge out of the old volcanic rocks.

We are off on a long sea voyage to Antarctica, at the southernmost end of the world. The vast Antarctic continent, covered by a mile-deep layer of ice, lies over and around the South Pole. It is encircled by wide seas and many large and small islands, and it is the coldest region on earth.

One of the exciting things about a voyage to Antarctica is that on the way we will pass places that scarcely any other human being has ever seen. It is like arriving in a different world, with limitless oceans on which you seldom meet other ships. Sometimes a great whale breaks the surface and sends a fountain of water shooting high in the air. White and blue-shadowed icebergs of every shape and size float, glittering, in the icy-cold, deep blue water.

Sometimes we see Antarctica's oddest inhabitants, the penguins, standing on these floating ice islands, looking like small human beings in black tailcoats and white shirts.

We are going to visit an island where penguins raise their young, and where few people have ever landed. Human beings could not live here, since it is almost entirely covered with ice and snow. This island, far out in the lonely Antarctic Ocean, is called Bouvet Island, after the Frenchman Jean Bouvet, who discovered it more than 250 years ago.

Lauritz Sømme
Sybille Kalas

The Penguin
Family
Book

Translated by Patricia Crampton

A MICHAEL NEUGEBAUER BOOK
NORTH-SOUTH BOOKS / NEW YORK / LONDON

Originally published in the United States, Canada, Great Britain, Australia, and New Zealand
by Picture Book Studio, Ltd. Reissued in paperback in 1995 by North-South Books,
an imprint of Nord-Süd Verlag AG.

Distributed in the United States by North-South Books Inc., New York.

Library of Congress Cataloging-in-Publication Data
Sømme, Lauritz
The Penguin Family Book.
Translation of: Das Pinguin-Kinder-Buch
Summary: Text and photographs portray a colony of Chinstrap penguins on Bouvet Island in the
Antarctic Ocean, from spring, when they lay their eggs, through summer, when the chicks hatch, to
autumn when they leave the island, until their return next spring.
1. Chinstrap penguin—Bouvet Island—Juvenile literature.
2. Chinstrap penguin—Bouvet Island—Behavior—Juvenile literature.
3. Birds—Bouvet Island—Juvenile literature.
4. Birds—Bouvet Island—Behavior—Juvenile literature.   [1. Chinstrap Penguin.   2. Penguins]
I. Kalas, Sybille.   II. Title
QL696.S473S5913 1988 598.4′41 87-32830

A CIP catalogue record for this book is available from The British Library.

ISBN 1-55858-379-3 (paperback) 10 9 8 7 6 5 4 3 2 1
Printed in Italy